Broke Entrepreneur:
Get mentally, emotionally, and physically prepared to start a business with little to no money.

Tashayla Williams, LCPC, NCC

Book Cover: Kevin D. Williams

E-book:

`ISBN-978-1-68418-152-0

Book:

ISBN-13: 978-1540505118

ISBN-10: 1540505111

DEDICATION

I dedicate this book to the entrepreneur that was told by themselves or others that their dreams were not possible.

Acknowledgements

This book is dedicated to my husband who was brave enough to be a #BrokeEntrepreneur with me, my mother, father, grandmother, brothers, sisters, nieces and nephew.

Editors: Helena Montfort, Marissa Puryear, Charisma Hodge and Anonymous.

CONTACT US:

Facebook: Life Embodied Therapy
Twitter: @lifeembodied
Instagram: @lifeembodiedtherapy
#BrokeEntreprenuer

"If you hear a voice within you saying
'you are not a painter,'
then, by all means, paint, and that voice will be
silenced."

- Vincent Van Gough

Table of Contents

Introduction

Do you awaken by your dreams each day? Have you ever had ideas that were so big that they seemed unattainable? Hello Entrepreneur, let's take this journey together.

Taking an idea from a thought to conceptualization can be challenging. When we are young, we are taught to attend school, obtain good grades, and get a job that will allow us to meet our basic needs. Socialized with these beliefs, we are not encouraged to consider the idea of finding a career that we enjoy. We are not encouraged to find a career that does not feel like work or one that feels like we have a purpose.

Society makes it acceptable to have a job that pays your bills and meets your basic needs, even if you are miserable. However, if you take the time to find a job that gives you purpose and a sense of belonging, you are unrealistic, a dreamer, and irresponsible. Friends and family members may look at you strangely if you tell them you are quitting your six-figured job, with benefits, to be an entrepreneur. You may even doubt your ability to be successful. However, you fear not trying more than you fear failing. You may lose relationships, material belongings, and the ability to settle for anything other than your purpose if you pursue entrepreneurship with little to no money. Stay focused 'Broke Entrepreneur', it will pay off.

In the journey toward entrepreneurship, you must be brave and consistently motivate yourself to move forward when things are going well and when they are not going well. Are you prepared? Before you begin incorporating your business and putting in the groundwork, you must get mentally, emotionally, and physically prepared to be a 'Broke Entrepreneur'

Dream

I envision your embrace
Like rain drops on my face
Unexpected but welcomed
To bring joy and to
Bring me through
A life of unfulfillment
To a life of contentment
With every sentiment
I await your presence
And with every lesson
I am wrestling
Between my heart and my mind
To find
That in which I'm searching
But reality is always lurking
Hurting
Going against what I was taught
To follow you
In hopes to reap the benefits soon
Because I cannot escape
The desire to make
Life seem worthwhile
And how I now smile
Because I'm awakened by the thought of you
Driven by your experience
And in remembrance
Of a time where I thought you were an option
Keeping me up at night
Pushing me through with all my might
Because I could not live a life so free
Without embracing the dreamer in me.

Tashayla Williams

Mental Preparation

"Logic will get you from A to B.
Imagination will take you everywhere".
-Albert Einstein

Identifying your Purpose

A leader should know what it means to follow, learn, remain curious, and take the opportunity to move forward with their dreams. Your purpose will derive from your worldview. Understanding your perspective of the world is essential to identifying your purpose. Spiritually, individuals define purpose as one's gift from a higher power. Others identify purpose as a concept that reflects a learned skill or expertise. Whatever your idea of purpose may be, do not stop seeking your purpose and dreaming. The moment you stop dreaming is the moment you stop living.

Close your eyes and imagine the world where you wake up excited every day. The world where you see opportunity through your eyes, feel excitement in your heart, smell the sweetest scent of contentment, hear your uninhibited laughter, and taste happiness in its entirety. Some people only imagine that these experiences can be a reality. Your reality may consist of fulfilling someone else's purpose. Every day you clock in, meet deadlines, or quotas. You may even minimize your abilities in anticipation of a promotion or a raise. Picture yourself getting a bonus based on drive rather than subjective work. You know it is time to make a change.

If you find yourself frustrated because you do not know your purpose, take some time to evaluate what you enjoy. Use each day as an opportunity to learn or explore something new. Whether, you take a cooking class, sewing class, business workshop, etc., these are experiences you can often find for "FREE", and will assist you with working toward your life's purpose. Use each day to move closer to a greater understanding of self. As you begin to explore your identity, you will have a greater understanding of your purpose and passion. Use the following prompts to identify if you have an entrepreneur mindset:

1) If you were in an empty room for 24 hours, what would you think about to occupy your mind?

2) What would you do to keep busy?

3) What is the one thing you enjoy doing no matter what mood you are in or how tired you may get?

4) What is going on when you are happiest?

5) Can you spend your life knowing that you are an entrepreneur and never give yourself a chance?

6) In your perfect world, how would your work day look?

7) Are you willing to sacrifice for your dreams?

Your responses to these questions will evoke you to have more questions, assure you that you are on the right career track and that you are not meant to be an entrepreneur, or make you question how you can start your journey as an entrepreneur. Use your responses as a Blueprint to finding your purpose or developing your purpose. As an entrepreneur, your options are limitless.

If you are a teacher, with an entrepreneur mindset, you can develop a school for children who have experienced trauma. If you are a lawyer, you can start a business defending the homeless. If you are an administrator, and have over 20 years of work experience, what is stopping you from opening your own Temporary Work Agency for administrators? No matter your expertise, entrepreneurship does not have any bounds. Explore your options and develop your identity as an entrepreneur.

I always knew I wanted to be a counselor. However, I wanted to be a counselor who was unique, with an identity that did not parallel what I knew about counseling. During my Master's in Mental Health Counseling program, there were many opportunities to explore my identity. At the time, I was not clear about how exploring my identity correlated with helping others. I found that it had everything do with helping others. How can I help others find and discover themselves if I am unsure of myself? I took this opportunity to not only develop as a counselor but also to develop as a person, who would later become a 'Broke Entrepreneur'.

One of the hardest tasks I had to complete in my counseling program was to receive a list of items I needed to learn about a client for a mocked counseling session. This mocked session was being evaluated by professors (who were members of the American Counseling Association). The purpose of the session was to determine if I could obtain information from clients in three minutes (without asking any questions). I am a straight forward person and became anxious at the idea of obtaining information without asking questions. I asked the professor to meet with me after class for a practice session.

During our practice sessions, I learned something about myself that I did not know impacted my worldview. As a child, I enjoyed singing, dance, and art. However, I viewed these activities as only hobbies. I was raised with the mindset that education was my primary focus. Thus, I looked at singing, dance, and art as something that was recreational. Fun was considered an optional part of my life. It went from optional to non-existent. Even though these things brought me joy, they were not included in my life daily. I became very emotional during the session. What was meant to be a mocked session became very real. I asked myself why am I still living my life without including activities I enjoy? I am an adult and I can choose how I want to live my life. From that day, I bought art materials and told myself I would include my interests in my life. Education was essential and important to assist me with honing my craft as a counselor. But, why shouldn't I be able to incorporate singing, dance, and art?

With this revelation, I attended another Master's class that was pivotal in developing my purpose. I selected this class without having a full understanding of what it entailed. This class was music therapy. The teacher asked, "When you think about how you would like to be remembered, what song comes to mind?" One of my classmates named a song that was familiar. I stated, "I love that song." The professor said, "Now sing the song." I thought the professor just wanted to hear the song. The other student and I sang the song. After we sung, the professor asked us to explain what we were thinking in the moment and how the song reflected our feelings through music. This experience was my introduction to expressive music therapy. It was at that time, I realized my purpose. I wanted others to experience that same feeling…fulfilment.

SACRIFICE

An entrepreneur is a person who organizes and operates a business or businesses, taking on greater than normal financial risks to do so. Being broke, in the sense of being an entrepreneur, means that you do not have savings, investors, or inheritance that can foster your dream. Lack of finances does not mean you cannot be an entrepreneur if you are willing to make sacrifices. LACK OF FINANCES DOES NOT MEAN YOU CAN NOT BE AN ENTREPRENEUR IF YOU ARE WILLING TO MAKE SACRIFICES!!! You will take even greater financial risks because you will sustain a greater loss than someone with assets.

Many individuals think it takes money to make money. If you are broke, ensure that you are rich in initiative, drive, and endurance. These characteristics are key elements of entrepreneurship. Do not, however, have a poor mentality. Having a poor mentality prevents you from evaluating ways to overcome being broke. A poor mentality consists of the inability to seek resources or look beyond one's finances. A poor mentality prevents you from developing tools and decreases your ability to implement sacrifices needed to succeed as a 'Broke Entrepreneur'.

Sacrifice is the key ingredient in preventing you from developing a 'poor mentality'. Mentally prepare to start your business. Depending on your financial situation, you will sacrifice a little or a lot, but there will be sacrifices. Some sacrifices can be as small as not eating out for a month to save the $125 to $200 to incorporate your business through your state's Department of Taxation. This process is usually completed online and takes five to ten minutes. Larger sacrifices may consist of choosing between, housing, car, or something vital to your business.

I know what you are thinking. I need somewhere to live. I need a car for transportation. As a 'Broke Entrepreneur', you must explore options. If you make temporary sacrifices, you will experience long term gain. Develop a plan to ensure that you are not making an aimless sacrifice. Sacrifices should not impede on your daily functioning. Implement sacrifices when you have a clear indication of why you are sacrificing.

Housing and transportation are among our basic needs. Identifying options to fulfill these basic needs can free up money for your business. If you have experienced being an independent adult, it will be difficult for you to sacrifice by living with someone else. If you have the option to stay with a friend, family member, or rent a room temporarily you may put yourself in a better position to accomplish your goals. These sacrifices may make you uncomfortable to visualize. Nevertheless, goal oriented temporary sacrifices may assist you with alleviating financial strain

If you have children, your sacrifices will look different. When I decided to be a 'Broke Entrepreneur', I did not have children. I know that my sacrifices would have been different if I had to consider children. You must incorporate their well-being and stability. Although, your sacrifices may look different when you have children, entrepreneurship is still attainable. In fact, you may have increased motivation because you have others who are dependent on your ability to make a dramatic change toward entrepreneurship. If your goal is to ensure long-term stability, a temporary sacrifice may be needed.

There are many affordable options that can prevent you from paying a hefty car note, insurance, repairs etc. Public transportation, Lyft, and Uber (or other ride options) may be sacrifices that assist you with starting your business. These options can free up money you would use for a car note. If you do not have to sacrifice your housing or transportation, you may have to sacrifice something that may prove to be more valuable, your time. Depending on what business you are looking to start, you must dedicate time that will go beyond what you have as a student, mom, dad, full-time worker, etc. Ask yourself, what do I need to sacrifice to start my business and what am I willing to sacrifice to start my business.

Before implementing sacrifices, you must clearly define your purpose. Your purpose should not include general statements such as "I just want to be my own boss" or "I just want to make a lot of money." Rather, your purpose should consist of specific statements such as, "I want to develop the first_____ and lead a team to accomplish _____." Being specific about your purpose will allow you to develop the motivation that you will need to mentally prepare to be an entrepreneur. Your purpose will act as a guide to the sacrifices you will need to take to be successful. As you explore the sacrifices that impact your business, make sure you are mentally prepared to take losses and gains. If you are not committed, you will waste time and effort. If your purpose is authentic and specific, you are prepared to sacrifice.

Many 'Broke Entrepreneurs' I have met shared similar stories of sleeping in their car, losing cars, not eating, having utilities cut off etc. I asked myself, why many entrepreneurs, who start a business with no money, share journeys where their sacrifices parallel. Housing, food, and transportation are often our largest bills. 'Broke Entrepreneurs' often sacrifice one, if not all, of these needs to implement their purpose. When I asked if they had any regrets, the answers were all the same. 'Broke Entrepreneurs' report that although they would have preferred not to have these experiences, it built perseverance and appreciation when they transitioned from being a 'Broke Entrepreneur'. Everyone may not have to experience these sacrifices. However, as insane as it sounds, these sacrifices are consistent among dreamers ('Broke Entrepreneurs') because quitting represented insanity as opposed to instability.

If someone asked me, before starting my business, what I would sacrifice for my business, I would have stated, "My time, my energy, and everything it takes." I would have made this statement, not realizing that it would take these things and more. I knew that there would be sacrifices. However, I did not know that I would gladly sacrifice things I would not imagine for my cause. When I decided to leave my job, where I was financially stable, I knew that it would be a sacrifice. I needed to complete my clinical for my Masters and was not able to work full-time, meet required internship hours for school, and start a business. I found an internship that paid me per client. It was flexible and allowed me the opportunity to make some money. However, I started with one client and was paid per session. The income that was needed to pay my bills was non-existent for a period. However, I had a purpose that required sacrifices.

MOTIVATION

So, you want to be your "own boss." What does that mean? Do you want to be your own boss because you lack the discipline to learn from others until you are ready to start your business? Do you just like the way it sounds to say "I am my own boss?" We often know that we are leaders and are entrepreneurs. However, if your sole goal is to make a lot of money, how will you survive the possibility of losing money? Making less money initially? Or not making any money? Entrepreneurship comes with many ups and downs. It requires that you make a commitment to yourself and your goals. Everyone has the potential to be an entrepreneur. However, everyone will not be an entrepreneur. Do you have potential or purpose?

When you are working to fulfill a purpose, you need to motivate yourself daily. Motivation can come in the form of daily affirmations, vision board, music, or whatever can inspire you. For some, experiencing doubt from others and having others question their decision to be an entrepreneur is motivation. The idea of knowing that others expect you to fail or do not think your dream is attainable can enable you to fight harder. There were not many people in my journey who were not encouraging or supportive. The few that were discouraging, I used as motivation. I knew that many individuals who are discouraging of other's dreams are often past dreamers. Only, they never woke up to pursue their dreams.

There were times where I felt discouraged and hoped that my sacrifices would pay off. As a 'Broke Entrepreneur', your natural supports are essential and can decrease budget constraints. One day, I sent my mother some ideas for her to develop advertisements. My mother would often complete my administrator work to support my decision to be a 'Broke Entrepreneur'. She responded in an email saying "You are about to blow up!" Now, for those of you wondering if my mother sent me a bomb threat over email, that is not what my mother intended to convey. "Blowing up" is a colloquialism for becoming famous or well known.

This phrase stuck with me. It derived from one of my favorite comedians, Martin Lawrence. Comedy is a tool I use for motivation. This statement reminded me that the sky was the limit. It was not my intention to become famous. I only wanted to evoke change that made me feel like I contributed to society. However, anytime I feel/felt discouraged I would say to myself "You are about to blow up." It makes me laugh and increases my motivation.

Motivation is key to identifying how you will you contribute to the world, your family, and friends, and society. Develop a plan to inspire yourself daily with self-care and encouragement. There will be days where you feel hopeless and wonder if it is worth being a 'Broke Entrepreneur'. Motivation feeds the drive you will need to keep going, even when things are moving slow or stagnant. Customize your motivation to specific goals you develop.

Initially, my goal was to develop a therapy practice that catered to the needs and individual issues of minority populations. Some daily motivations I incorporated was listening to inspirational music, researching about successful therapy practices, and reading about barriers that prevent minorities from using therapy as a tool to overcome life challenges. These tools kept me focused on my goal and assisted me with processing what my contribution would look like as an entrepreneur. My motivation derived from my desire to go against the norm. Work, a place where you spend most of your time, should be a place where you can be creative and should foster your professional growth.

If your goal is to own a beauty salon, let your daily motivation consist of ways to reach your goal. Use each day to identify ways to make your salon unique by catering to special populations. Let's say you want to start a catering business, you can motivate yourself by enrolling in a culinary arts course or researching new recipes to try each week. If you are looking to start a tax business, motivate yourself to learn ways to make tax preparation a comfortable and informative experience. Whatever, you decide to do, find ways to motivate yourself daily. Preferably, find free ways to motivate yourself daily. Use research, local event websites, or papers as tools to identify free ways to increase motivation. Remember, you are a 'Broke Entrepreneur' and every cent counts.

RESILIENCE

You cannot be fearful of the word "No." You should be more fearful of the phrase "I did not try." When starting my business, I found myself so excited that I just wanted to hurry up and get to the finish line of success. I would attempt to collaborate and pursue individuals who were vital to making my business successful. I wanted them to know that I was persistent and that I was worth taking a chance. Sometimes, individuals responded well and appreciated that I was confident. Others, viewed my attempt to demonstrate confidence, as overwhelming and aggressive. Maybe I was, at times, being too aggressive. I was finding my way.

Eventually, you will learn how to evaluate individual's responses and to identify boundaries when working to make business connections. When you are looking to connect or network with an organization, research, research, research. Research to determine what communication approach would work best. You must be resilient and balance confidence with cockiness. Additionally, you must balance initiative with resilience.

One day, I attempted to contact an organization to share my services. During this time, I received funding through a grant and I needed organizations to agree to allow me to conduct services. I secured two contracts from other organizations. I was excited! I thought "Let's try to get a third organization on board." My attempt did not go over well. I researched and understood the dynamics of the organization. I identified the point of contact to obtain a contract. I knew that contacting him would be difficult. I left two messages and did not receive a response. Some individuals prefer persistence to make sure you are serious. I did not think twice about making several attempts to reach out to the point of contact weekly. When I finally got in touch with the contact for the organization, he stated, "Yes, I received ALL of your messages and attempts to contact me. We are not interested."

It was at that moment, I realized I may have pushed too hard. Being a 'Broke Entrepreneur' will do that for you. You think that you must move quickly and aggressively to be successful. Balance is key. Be confident and let organizations know that you are interested, without seeming desperate. Some people and companies may not want to network or entertain your idea. It is ok. Once you focus on those who are willing to take a chance on you, others will seek you out. Don't make lemonade out of lemons. Make lemon cake as you dance in your lemon colored shoes, to the beat of your own lemon shaped drum. Do not let rejection stop your process. Maintain resilience.

ASSERTIVENESS

Communication is essential to being a 'Broke Entrepreneur'. Whether you are discussing your business with a potential partner or a potential investor, assertiveness will play a role in preparing you to be an entrepreneur. Assertiveness is the act of communicating in a calm and positive manner. If you are passive about your business, others will not view your business as being important. If you are passive aggressive, you will be viewed as unsure. If you are too aggressive, you will appear to "Know it all" and to not be a team player.

Convey that you are confident and knowledgeable. Also, present eager to learn and to partner. Before entering a meeting or making a phone call, ask yourself, "How do I want them to view my business?" "How do I want them to view me as an Entrepreneur?" Then, ensure your conversations and interactions are a representation of how you would like to be perceived. You may be a 'Broke Entrepreneur', but your conversations and interactions can provide opportunities that have no value (priceless). Prior to, during, and after becoming a 'Broke Entrepreneur', your communication will impact your success.

Entrepreneur Communication Categories

Whether you decide to embark on entrepreneurship or not, you will communicate with your verbal or non-verbal actions that you are, indeed, an entrepreneur. It is essential for you to identify where you fall in the 'Entrepreneur Communication Categories.' These categories not only provide insight into your communication style but it allows you to evaluate how you are perceived by others when you do not fulfil your dreams. The 'Entrepreneur Communication Categories' reflect my understanding of the role communication plays in our daily lives. I developed the

'Entrepreneur Communication Categories' based on my experiences with individuals who expressed interest in being an entrepreneur by incorporating their verbal and non-verbal cues. Evaluate the characteristics of each communication category to see if any the characteristics resonate.

'Passive Entrepreneur'

You know your purpose but do not feel that you can risk taking a chance on your purpose. You know you should follow your dream. You do not make any attempts to explore or create an opportunity to become an entrepreneur. You see others doing similar work and wonder what how it would feel for you to do the same thing. However, you are not moved to put your thoughts into action. Passive Entrepreneurs experience a lot of self-talk. "I would like to own a barbershop." "I wish I could sell my fashion designs." You have the mind to create, take risks, and make a mark. However, you are content with only imagining a world where your purpose is fulfilled. However, you are obviously living in a world where you are unfulfilled.

'Passive Aggressive Entrepreneur'

Next, is the 'Passive Aggressive Entrepreneur'. You have ideas and an outlook of your purpose. However, you fear taking a chance. Your fear evokes you to look down on others or to make discouraging statements like, "If I started a restaurant business, I would have cold cuts on hoagie bread and not sliced bread." Why didn't you start your business? This risk was "too great", and you are resentful. At some point, you may even engross yourself in someone else's business as if it were your business. You may even take over the business because you have boundary issues.

'Aggressive Entrepreneur'

As an 'Aggressive Entrepreneur', you know your purpose. You think everyone else should "Know" your purpose too. To that end, you have unrealistic expectations of other's ability to support you financially or emotionally. You are entitled. Your arrogance clouds your ability to be humbly confident. Everyone owes you and should be happy that you are willing to share yourself, your ideas, and your purpose with the world.

'Assertive Entrepreneur'

As an assertive entrepreneur, you recognize your ability to implement your ideas. You take every opportunity to fulfill your goals. You know that you do not have all the answers, but you are willing to learn from others. You may or may not lack finances to start a business. However, finances are not a factor in your desire to fulfill your purpose. You are willing to sacrifice, and you are equipped with a willingness to develop mentally, emotionally and physically as an entrepreneur.

If you have fallen into any category other than an 'Assertive Entrepreneur', ask yourself, "Why not?" Evaluate the barriers that prevent you from taking your journey toward entrepreneurship. Then, evaluate if you can see yourself living with an entrepreneur mindset and not developing to your full potential. It is not easy to take an idea or concept and put it into action. However, if you find yourself exhibiting characteristics of a 'Passive Entrepreneur', 'Passive Aggressive Entrepreneur' or an 'Aggressive Entrepreneur.' you will not only resent your life decisions but you will find yourself in a constant state of discouragement, even anger. Anger within yourself for not thinking that your dreams were worth the sacrifice.

An experience where I exercised assertiveness was with a potential funder. I submitted a grant application and received a letter stating that the potential funder was interested in my project. However, they wanted to make site visits and follow the progress of my program for a year before they decided to give me a grant. I would have ignored the letter and not followed up with the organization as a passive communicator. "I do not know why you didn't fund me, but thank you for your consideration" is an example of passive aggressive communication. "What is wrong with you, I should have gotten this award?" is an aggressive communication response.

Instead, I contacted the president and inquired about improvements to my proposal. I invited him to observe my expressive music therapy group. The gentleman met with me to conduct a site visit. He entered a prison for the first time and interacted with several of the group members. After his experience, he stated, "I read your proposal and I tried to imagine your program. However, nothing could prepare me for this amazing experience. I enjoyed what I saw and will be recommending you for funding." This experience taught me to offer all potential funders the ability to see the program in person. Also, I implemented a more visual outlook of the program through my grant proposal writing. Assertiveness is a key factor to mentally prepare you to be a 'Broke Entrepreneur.'

Emotional Preparation

"Your time is limited
so, don't waste it living someone else's life.
-Steve Jobs

Perceive, understand, manage, and use your emotions as you prepare to be an entrepreneur. Some emotions are feelings that we cannot control. Others emotions act as supports and should be implemented as coping tools. Do not be afraid of the emotions you feel on this journey. Embrace your emotions and process them in a healthy manner. Use natural or professional supports, as needed. You will need to be emotionally prepared to be a 'Broke Entrepreneur'.

COURAGE

My entire life my grandmother would say a quote from Shakespeare. I did not understand what it meant until I became an adult. The quote states, "Cowards die many times before their deaths. The valiant never taste of death but once Julius Caesar (II, ii, 32-37)." Its meaning derives from the idea that at some point in our lives we must be courageous. Lack of courage evokes a lack of production, which feeds stagnation. To be stagnant is to die figuratively. No matter how many mistakes you make, you should live your life courageously, with no regrets. Deciding to start a business as a 'Broke Entrepreneur' is not a courageous act within itself. Courageously taking steps to implement your business will assist you to, as Shakespeare states, "Never taste death but once."

An entrepreneur once told me that there was a partnership she wanted to develop for her organization. The entrepreneur reported that she offered the company she wanted to partner with one month of free work. She informed them that if they did not want to partner with her after the month, she would leave with no expectations. However, she stated that if they wanted to proceed forward, after the one month period, they would need to offer her a contract. It takes courage when you are a 'Broke Entrepreneur.' You may wonder how you will make money if you are giving away services for free. Don't look at it as giving away services for free. Look at it as investing in and marketing yourself. By being courageous, this entrepreneur expanded and developed a brand that has afforded her opportunities that may not have been available if she would have responded, "Their loss" or "They are going to have to pay me." Courage can open a floodgate of opportunities that will impact your success.

If you find yourself wondering why you cannot take a chance on yourself or an idea, evaluate the underlying fears associated with this belief. Explore your inability to be courageous. Some individuals are unable to be courageous because they fear being successful. Is this you? Sometimes our life experiences inform our ability to experience happiness and to take chances. If you find yourself feeling that you do not deserve to be happy, you fear becoming successful, or are concerned about not being successful, work to increase feelings of self-worth. We all experience fear and may have some inadequacies. However, if you do not love yourself enough to be courageous, through your dreams, others will see and feel your fear. Some may support you with reducing that fear. Many will perceive it as weakness or a lack of confidence. Lack of courage will negatively impact the opportunities you may have as a 'Broke Entrepreneur.' Be courageous.

ANXIETY

The anxiety experience as a 'Broke Entrepreneur' will not parallel to the anxiety you will already experience as a start-up business. Every cent you spend will be accounted for and will impact your daily living. Losing money may feel like the end of the world. Anxiety will enter, but you must be prepared to conquer anxiety.

Being a 'Broke Entrepreneur' ignited my faith and resilience. I feared being broke, potential failure, and investing too much. Every time I began to have a negative thought, God reminded me that he (or she) was still present. There were times I wanted to give up but would always be reminded through a person, inspirational word, or opportunity (I did not seek or ask for) that my work was not in vain. The DSM-IV (Diagnostic Statistical Manual), used in counseling and psychology, defines anxiety as extreme worry, feeling keyed up, trouble sleeping, trouble concentrating, and an inability to stay focused. Anxiety can be used to enhance your start-up or can be detrimental. To conquer anxiety, identify what informs your anxiety.

Are you worried about your finances? How others will view your decision to be a 'Broke Entrepreneur'? Are you simply worried about not knowing if you will be successful? I experienced each one of these at different periods. You have one life and one shot to make the most out of your life. No one wants to be broke. However, you will quickly realize that, where finances help you to sustain a certain lifestyle, it will come secondary to other gains you will accomplish as an entrepreneur.

Individuals you know may have knowledge that you are starting a business with little to no assets or investments. Their limited knowledge of business will evoke them to wonder how you can start a business without assets or investments. Undoubtedly, the people who have an opinion will not be entrepreneurs. Some individuals fall under the categories of 'Passive Entrepreneur', 'Passive Aggressive

Entrepreneur' or 'Aggressive Entrepreneur'. This unique lifestyle is not for everyone and it is ok for them to have their opinion. You, however, must make sure that these opinions do not impact your end goals. Doubt may occur. You must combat each doubt with your customized motivation techniques; cognitively restructuring any negative thoughts.

Thinking too hard of the possibility of not being successful is maladaptive to the process of entrepreneurship. Rather, you should spend your time making decisions, networking, and developing your business to ensure that you will be successful. I recommend creating a calendar. On the calendar, write a task to complete each day that contributes to the development of your business. For example, your calendar may have a week where you contact a congress member every day to build a network of supporters. Maybe another week you can spend each day writing parts of a five to ten- year business plan. Do not sell yourself short. Again, I say, DO NOT SELL YOURSELF SHORT!!!

I contacted some famous artists and musicians to support my program, build credibility, seek opportunities for financial support, and obtain opportunities for my clients returning to communities from prison. I figured if individuals are given opportunities to explore talents and interests, criminal behaviors would decrease. I found that many well-known individuals had managers who are accessible by retrieving their numbers from Google. Many artists and musicians are philanthropists and they look for creative ways to give back to communities.

There's a part of me that wondered, "Why would they want to talk to me?" I am not well-known. I often doubted my ability to make connections. However, contacting these potential contacts would assisted me with having an opportunity to practice networking and to make connections. I knew I was a 'Broke Entrepreneur' and that I needed to seek opportunities to sustain my program after my funding ran out. Coping with anxiety during this process is not easy. Life will happen. Things may get tough, but again, you must be more fearful of not trying, than trying.

PRIDE

Pride can decrease your ability to be successful. I like to think of myself as a social loner. I enjoy being around others. However, regarding business, I would prefer to work alone. However, this is not the best way to be successful. If there are people or companies who are vital to your success, ASK FOR HELP! Every business owner needs a network.

Initially, I was hesitant to reach out to other therapists or clinics to ask for advice or to network. I wondered if it would be a conflict of interest because they were in the same line of work. However, I realized that although we were in the same line of work, I had a specialty interest (the forensic population) that every therapist was not interested in pursuing. Many seasoned therapists I encountered were supportive and gave me insight into things I did not know about the business side of being a therapist.

One day, I was feeling anxious about starting my first program. I made several unsuccessful attempts to network with organizations. I received an email from an organization within my network to participate in a conference. The conference was sponsored by an organization in which I was interested in partnering with for my program. At the bottom of the email, I saw the name of someone I worked with briefly at another institution. I thought, this will be an opportunity to inquire about collaborating with her to partner with her institution. I wondered if I should contact the individual directly to see if she remembered me and could attest to my character and work ethic.

It had been years since I worked with this individual and I was unsure if she would remember me. After realizing how much I would regret not trying, I mustered up the courage to send her an email. I attempted what would be the jumpstart to implementing my program. In the email, I introduced myself, described my program, and shared that we worked together previously. Immediately, I received a response. Not only did she remember me, but also, she introduced me to someone who oversaw programs at her institution.

I started my first program based on that email interaction in less than a few weeks. I am telling this story not only to remind you that pride should go out the door, but also to share that relationships that you have and will build on this journey will greatly impact your success and your opportunities. If I did not initiate an email, it would have been very challenging for me to start entering prisons as an independent contractor, with no business history with their organization.

When you allow the emotional pride to influence your journey toward entrepreneurship, it can be detrimental. It can be difficult to ask for help. However, as a 'Broke Entrepreneur', asking for help can open doors, increase finances, and assist you with building lasting relationships. I found that when you are transparent with others, they are often willing to support your cause. No one wants to appear broke or financially unstable. Nevertheless, if you set your pride aside and communicate your situation with individuals, who are looking to invest or who are willing to take a chance on your business, doors will open. Decreasing pride is an act that is free. Maintaining a prideful spirit can cause you to incur costs that you do not need as a 'Broke Entrepreneur'.

PATIENCE

Patience is an emotion that will need to be apparent as a 'Broke Entrepreneur.' Developing patience may not be easy. We live in a world where we can obtain many things very quickly. If we have an inkling that something is not going to develop quickly, we often run or decline to pursue. You should prepare yourself to have patience.

Initially, I received grant money and had to find organizations that would agree to let me conduct my program at their institution. Individuals would appear excited about the program, ask me to send information, and would not follow through. I understood their hesitation to implement a new program. However, I was receiving declinations more frequently than I anticipated. I thought, "I am not asking them to pay for my work. I am coming with my own funding. What is the problem?" My motivation, at that point, was to demonstrate to those who invested in me that they did not make a mistake. I continued to network and pursue opportunities. I started three programs in two states in the same week. Initially, I only wanted to start with one program. However, I had the opportunity to provide more services. I found that I needed to trust God, have faith, and patience on this journey. Your individual belief system will play a huge role daily.

Prior to starting three programs in one week, I excitedly anticipated a meeting with a liaison who could determine if I started my program in all institutions for my state. At the end of the meeting, I was left wondering if my goals would ever be accomplished. I was told that my program was great and would be an excellent way to reduce recidivism. Then, I was informed of their ambivalence. The state did not know my organization and needed to build a relationship. I would be remised if I did not say, at times, I felt discouraged. However, I remained patient. I looked for other opportunities to develop my program, to establish a relationship, and to be persistent. After months of patience, I developed a partnership and established a relationship with the state liaison.

Time is a commodity as a 'Broke Entrepreneur.' Entrepreneurship is a process that requires time and patience. If you find that you cannot sacrifice or invest full time in your business, dedicate a time to work on your business daily. Whether it is an hour, three hours, or four hours a day when you are working to build your business, patience is key. The amount of work you put into your business may determine the amount of patience you will need to see your business develop. Although you may want things to happen immediately, that is not how entrepreneurship works. You may become frustrated with being patient as a 'Broke Entrepreneur.' You will think of bills, credit, and maybe even material belongings. Are these things replaceable? You can always re-build your credit or obtain new material items. However, opportunity, may not be replaceable.

HAPPINESS

When I began my journey as a 'Broke Entrepreneur,' I was not sure what happiness would look like for me. I only knew I had these ideas that would keep me up at night and wondered if I would ever see it come to fruition. In July 2014, I decided that I was going to work to implement one of my ideas. As a licensed therapist, it was my passion to increase other's idea of mental health supports and to develop a program where therapy did not feel like therapy. I also wanted to combine my interests with my expertise.

I began researching how to write a grant proposal. Many sites recommended that entrepreneurs hire grant writers. I knew, however, that I was a 'Broke Entrepreneur' and I could not afford to hire a grant writer. I began researching million-dollar grant proposals. I evaluated language, format, etc. to develop my first grant proposal. On

September 2014, I was sent a check for $30,000 from Wells Fargo. The check I received was the most I had seen at one time in my then 27 years of life. My happiness, at this point, was not only due to receiving a check but it was also due to having a corporate foundation believe in my idea enough to offer support. I had to process the fact that something that I only imagined was about to come true. That feeling, at that moment, was happiness.

I developed the Offender To Returning Citizen-Transition Program, a program that provides expressive art and music therapy in jail and prisons. The program was developed to reduce recidivism by increasing mental health supports. Remember, I mentioned previously that some people think that it takes money to make money. Well, it does take money to make money. However, it does not have to be your money. Use your resources. I wrote this initial grant proposal while having -$5 in my bank account. I left a job where I was financially stable to invest in myself. Making this sacrifice was not easy. However, this temporary sacrifice assisted me with obtaining long term gain.

See, what some people do not understand is that when you do not have initial financial support, it evokes you to have a drive that money cannot buy. You wake up with a hunger to succeed that may be both figurative and literal.

Ambition is driven by hope and faith. I do not know what it means to be an entrepreneur with assets. However, not having assets assisted me with building perseverance. This perseverance enabled me to continue working toward my dream each day. I knew I wanted to create and implement change. I used, what some would call a deficit, as motivation. Even if I had gotten check for $5 to support my project, I would have been happy. Your happiness, as an entrepreneur, will look different than others. Every step you take will provide an unexplainable happiness that will carry you throughout your journey.

I challenge you to evaluate what happiness looks like for you personally and relating to your business. Write it down so you do not forget. Then, with each milestone of your journey, write down experiences that have made you happy. Every step of your journey will allow you to experience happiness in a way you would have never imagined. I recall happiness when others would become intrigued by hearing about my business. When I networked with an individual I respected told me my idea was "Genius", I felt happiness. Happiness is an emotion you will feel when you discover resources that take the place of finances. Define your happiness and work to exceed your expectations.

Physical Preparation

"Formal education will make you a living; self-education will make you a fortune." -Jim Rohn

MONEY/INVESTMENTS

Grants

As I stated, my business start-up fund came from applying for a grant. If you have attended college or used a grant for private schools, you may be familiar with the fact that grants are funds that you do not have to pay back. However, when it comes to grants for programs and projects, there is more accountability and it is very competitive. First, you must have a clear idea what you want to do. Grants are not given just to open a business. Further, you must be a non-profit to obtain grants. If you are not a non-profit, you can obtain fiscal sponsorship from a non-profit. You may obtain a fiscal sponsorship while you are establishing your non-profit or as a long-term partnership.

You are only allowed to use grants for certain projects. You cannot seek a grant to open a beauty shop. However, you can seek a grant that caters to children and adults with disabilities; allowing them to have reasonable accommodations while being serviced. You cannot ask funders to open a tax business but you can seek funding for financial literacy for teens and young adults. Funders are philanthropists who are looking to invest in extraordinary projects.

Prior to seeking grant funding, you must research to see if your project is eligible for a grant. Once you have determined it is eligible for a grant, begin outlining your program or project. If you are not skilled at writing and can afford a grant writer, this could be helpful. However, if you are a 'Broke Entrepreneur' and have some writing skills, began researching grants that are awarded in your area of interest. There are free pdfs of grant proposals that are awarded online. These free resources can assist you with understanding grant proposal format and grant proposal language. I found that the 'Baltimore Common Grant Application Format' is a format that translates to any proposal that you will submit to any organization. After you have completed your proposal in this format, you can use it to apply for any grant if you are eligible.

Stocks

If you find that your business does not qualify for grant funding, explore your options. Consider partnering with someone who has assets and are willing to invest in your ideas or concepts. Additionally, you can purchase stocks for as little as $5 to $10 per share. You can purchase some shares, let it mature, and take it out when you are ready to start your business. You can meet with a professional at your local bank to discuss ways to minimally invest for your future as an entrepreneur. Give yourself a timeline and educate yourself about your options. You can meet with a banker to discuss options for free. Also, you can obtain an App on your phone or other electronic device that tells you the costs of stocks for free.

Get Creative

You can independently fundraise using your skills and talents. If you are an artist, sell your paintings and artwork. If you can sing, you can sell tickets to fundraise for your business with a solo concert. Use your profits to start your business. If you make a tasty lemon moraine pie, sell pies to assist you with funding your business. While you're at it, open a pie business as a second income.

One entrepreneur, who has a criminal background. returned home from prison. He wanted to make a change. Although this entrepreneur wanted to make a change, he did not know how to make money, outside of selling drugs.

He began selling dinners that were made from food he would cook for himself. Eventually, he started getting requests and obtaining contracts to cater to several businesses. He temporarily sacrificed food he bought for his household to invest in his business. This 'Broke Entrepreneur' did not allow lack of money to stop him from pursuing entrepreneurship. Instead, he used his limited assets to develop a now very successful business. Remember to challenge yourself to think outside the box.

IN-KIND SUPPORT

There are several organizations that offer in-kind support to non-profits. In-kind supports are donations. In-kind supports are a great way to seek items for free. Most times, you only need to submit your non-profit status letter. If you are looking to start an after-school program for children, you may be able to receive in-kind supports from your local grocery store or department store. These stores may be able to supply healthy after-school snacks or supplies. Additionally, if you have a fundraiser and are looking for items to auction, local sports teams, and local restaurants often give away in-kind items or gift certificates to non-profit organizations. Exploring these options reduces the cost of items that would come out of your budget. It also provides you with opportunities to network with community organizations.

One of the ways I have fundraised for my organization was through auctions. If you are going to conduct an auction, allow yourself time to plan and obtain items that people would want to purchase. In-kind items can be used at auctions. You do not have to pay for items and you receive a profit from items that are purchased. If items are not purchased, you do not lose any money. If you are looking to receive in-kind support for an after-school program, you may want to invite the staff or corporate members of the local grocery store to your auction. Then, allow the participants of the after-school program to show off their talents or something they learned from the program. This is a free way to advertise and to obtain ongoing support. Supporters love to see where they are making their investments.

Some organizations will not list that they offer in-kind supports to organizations. They may not even understand what it means to offer in-kind supports to organizations. Never hesitate to contact an organization you think would be interested in supporting you to inquire about their ability or desire to offer support.

Keep in mind, we live in a world where individuals may not give you something for nothing. Offer a service or recognition to supporters or investors. When receiving in-kind supports, I found that organizations were happy to learn that they would be listed on my website or other public access sites. Acknowledging your in-kind supports increases their exposure, communicates that they support worthy causes, and that they give back to communities. The best part is that it does not cost you any money to inquire. Also, it does not cost you money to offer acknowledgement.

NETWORKING/SOCIAL MEDIA

I recall speaking with a funder who inquired about my website and whether I was on social media. At the time, I had a Facebook page I used once a year. However, the funder explained that some investors or funders would view your social media and website to see if and how often you are interacting with the public. Social media is especially helpful if your business consists of working with the community or outreach. I went from using my social media once a year to using it every day to report project progress, to establish a social media presence for my business, and to develop a network. Through social media, I advertise for positions, interact with other entrepreneurs, and share updates.

While thinking about how to continue to develop my program. I asked myself, how can I expand services for my program? I wanted to assist clients with increasing coping skills through art and music therapy. Additionally, I wanted to assist my clients with having employment options. Many of my client's crimes were committed to provide for themselves financially. I knew there was a need for employment options.

I found myself watching a reality TV show (yes reality TV is my guilty pleasure). I saw that the owner of a tattoo shop giving individuals with artistic abilities the opportunity to use their skills as a means of income. The opportunity the owner provided gave them an option that was a positive alternative to engaging in a life of crime. I was intrigued. I started following the owner on social media and saw that his manager was listed in his bio. I sent an email to his manager and shared my program. I asked to meet to discuss a partnership. The manager was very open and was happy that I reached out to collaborate. Again, this is something that was out of the norm for my personality. However, my ambition enabled me to reduce the fear and anxiety that came with the unknown.

Initially, I thought the reason I was contacting the manager was to collaborate with his client. After having patience (1 year), I found that the manager was someone in which I needed to partner with for my business for other reasons. I followed the manager on social media. I saw the manager was very busy with going out of the country, managing, and directing. I thought, "He would not possibly want to collaborate or partner with me because I am not famous or well known."

One day, I felt motivated. I thought "You are not famous or well known, but you have a worthy cause and can potentially increase opportunities for your clients with this partnership." I contacted the manager and learned that we shared several interests. Additionally, he was open to offering support and assisting with developing and expanding my program. The manager was also someone who had a dream and did not have initial assets. He took a chance on himself and was willing to give back. He is very successful because he does not forget the sacrifices he had to make to pursue his dreams. Currently, we are working to develop our partnership. This opportunity was only possible through networking.

Facebook

Facebook is a free social media tool that can assist you with networking with other business owners, potential partnerships, and investors. Make sure your business page is separate from your personal page. If you find yourself mixing your business page and your personal page, it may communicate that you do not have a "real business" and that you do not know how to differentiate between business and personal.

If you have some videos of yourself singing but mostly selfies or pictures of your family, how will someone view you as a singer? Viewers may think, "Wow, he has a great family but I do not see much of his talent." Rather, create a free separate business page where you are only showing your music talents. As a 'Broke Entrepreneur', you will depend on every free resource as an opportunity. I am guilty of not posting as often as I should on my business page. However, you should make it clear and simple for others to differentiate business and personal on your Facebook page.

Twitter

Twitter is a great way to network and obtain exposure for your business. Again, make sure if you are going to post about your plumbing business one day, you do not turn around and post that you are "Mad at your girlfriend" and that "People should learn to be loyal". What does this have to do with plumbing? We all experience our personal ups and downs. However, sharing these experiences in public outlets can negatively impact your business and money you do not have as a 'Broke Entrepreneur'. Twitter is an awesome way to contact others around the world. Dream big! If you are a plumber and a Madonna fan, why not attempt to contact her on Twitter about her plumbing needs. After all, what do you have to lose? Use Twitter as a tool try ideas that may sound crazy and outrageous.

Instagram

Instagram is another free social media tool where you can post pictures or videos to tell a story. Individuals should be able to view your Instagram and understand your business. Find opportunities to share experiences, share your work, or to post videos about business. Instagram not only allows you to network but it caters to visual learners who may receive more about your business through videos and pictures

Social media is an evolving tool that will yield more opportunities for exposure. Although, these outlets for exposure may not always be around, the concepts remain the same if they are added to or replaced. Use these free resources to show the process of your journey, to develop your business, and to network. If your business is creating a new form of social media, use the existing tunnels to expose and share your business. While social media remains free or reasonably priced, it is an essential tool to the success of a 'Broke Entrepreneur.'

ADVERTISING AS A 'BROKE ENTREPRENEUR'

Ask yourself, what are your advertisement needs and what ways you can ensure little to no cost. Business cards, pamphlets, radio interviews, and apparel are ways to bring light to your business. These items can range from free to very expensive. Identify your non-monetary resources. Do you know someone who has access to a commercial printer or who would trade artistic expressions for something you can offer? You are a 'Broke Entrepreneur' and need to assess how you can advertise in the cheapest way possible.

Business Cards

I needed to offer a way for individuals to contact me about business. I knew that business cards would cost money that I could not afford to invest. I researched and found an organization that offered 50 free business cards. I immediately ordered the free business cards and used the cards as my first advertisements for my business. Research sites that provide free business cards. These sites will send you free business cards as an incentive to get you will buy other advertisement items. You can also create business cards using several free templates online.

Pamphlets and Brochures

Although professionally made pamphlets are nice in appearance, they can be very costly and not in your budget as a 'Broke Entrepreneur.' Try Microsoft Publisher or Word where you can explore several options for brochure templates. This will provide you will a more affordable option. People will pay more attention to the content of your brochure as opposed to what card stock and gloss you use. Additionally, you can contact local organizations, introduce your business, tell them that you are working on a limited budget. Offer the organization a service or tell them you will advertise them as supporters of your cause on social media or your website for discounts or in-kind pamphlet or brochure copies.

Other Advertisements

Many office supply stores and online supply stores sell car magnets for $15 or less. Individuals can retrieve information about your business when you are sleeping and your car is parked. You can also create hats, t-shirts, and other apparel by going to Walmart and or Michaels. Write or creatively display your business name or website on apparel for advertisement. I once bought hats from Walmart for $2, paint for 98 cents and a stencil for $2 to advertise. If you are not crafty, please utilize Pinterest or YouTube as ways to increase knowledge about how to use crafts to advertise for a reasonable price.

Events

Look at your community calendar or inquire about special events at schools that may benefit from your business and services. There may be a community event about affordable health care. If you have a business providing free medical screenings for adults, attending an event like this can increase your networks and assist you with developing notoriety for your business. Look for events that are free for vendors. If an event is not free, vendor registrations are usually reasonably priced and are worth the exposure. You can establish business relationships and clients by attending the event.

Radio/Television

Find ways to network, make connections, and to bring light to your program. One of the ways you can do this for free is through radio or podcast interviews. Many radio stations and podcasts have segments where they interview local businesses. These interviews are free and give you a lot of public exposure. If you are interested in obtaining worldwide exposure, you should sign up for RadioGuestList.com. This site sends daily recommendations for radio and podcast interviews. These recommendations not only lead up to potential customers but it also provides the opportunity for you to network with other professionals.

Do not be afraid to contact television shows and news broadcasts to share your business. Many of these organizations seek new innovative ideas and businesses. What do you have to lose? A way to advertise for free?

Potential network opportunity? Go for it! Maybe you can call a radio or television station once a day for a week. Obtain radio or media exposure as a tool to maintain ambition and contribute to the development of your business.

Business Office

I have spoken with several aspiring business owners who informed me that the only thing stopping them from starting a business is their credit or inability to pay for a commercial leasing space. I also had this concern. I wondered how I would pay for a commercial space without a savings or investments. There are several options. First, ask yourself do I have a clientele? How many days a week/hour will I need to start my business? You have options for free or low cost co-working spaces all over the world.

Among the best web sites to obtain reasonable office space for as little as an hour, to days, or months without a long-term lease is www.liquidspace.com. Many spaces on this site are free or low cost. These spaces give you an opportunity to have meetings without having to commit to a long-term lease and pay a ridiculous amount for your monthly rent. If you do not have clients or participants for your business, do not commit to a long-term lease. Start small and build your business before you obtain a permanent space. You are a 'Broke Entrepreneur' and need to ensure that you grow as your business grows to prevent debt or loss.

Business Materials

If your business requires materials, this can impact money allocated for your household. For example, if you are a dancer and you require tap shoes or ballet shoes, these items may pose an expense you cannot afford as a 'Broke Entrepreneur.' You must set your pride aside and explore resources. Inquire about used or unused materials at a dance studio or dance school. Offer free services in exchange for materials you may need. Even though you are broke, the only thing you cannot afford is not attempting to pursue your goals.

Evaluating Free Resources

Before you buy crayons for your daycare center, research programs that offer in-kind donations. When contacting organizations that have items you may need, be specific. Although an organization may not advertise that they give away free resources, the organization may make accommodations if you make an inquiry and describe your cause. Also, you can obtain free resources in your area or utilize craigslist's "Free Stuff" section to seek furniture, instruments, toys decorations etc. or other items that may contribute to your business to assist with reducing costs.

GROWING YOUR BUSINESS

Your business can grow as much as you work. If you intend to have a viable business, you should never stop thinking about ways to grow.

One day I was thinking about ways to grow my business. I could not help but wonder what it would look like for my program to be one of the largest jails and most well-known jails in the United States. The next day, I called the largest and most violent jail in the United States. I retrieved a contact for community partnerships. I was curious about what response I would receive if I shared about my program. After speaking with the liaison, I was asked to send information via email to describe my program.

A week later, I was asked to attend a meeting to discuss my program. At the meeting, the liaison offered me the opportunity start my program immediately. Now, some may read this and say this does not sound real. Well, believe me, it did not feel real. I had confidence in my program but thought expanding to another state was a long-term goal. The feeling was unexplainable and it is not comparable to any other experience. This was my first lesson in dreaming big.

What does growing your business look like for you? Whether you want to stay local, expand to other states, countries or continue to grow, growing your business will allow you to maintain financially stability and momentum. No dream is too big, no goal is out of reach.

Multiple Businesses

If you are looking to grow your business, create a plan. Sometimes, businesses can flourish grow faster than expected. Take your time to understand the responsibilities that come with having multiple businesses. Work to establish one business at a time. Evaluate your motivation and potential sacrifices for developing another business. Is this another venture in which you are passionate? If you are working to develop your business and you are selling pies, (from our previous example), you can establish a business selling pies as well. If you are mentally capable of maintaining multiple businesses, do so.

Multiple Locations

When you obtain multiple locations for your business, you not only increase exposure, but again, you increase responsibilities. If you are looking to expand your business in multiple locations, you have two options for establishing your business in other states or countries. You can establish a branch of your business with a new name, extending it to a specific location. You can also establish your business as a foreign entity, while maintaining your business in the primary location your business was incorporated. Ask yourself, is my business financially ready to expand to different locations. As you expand to different locations, you must maintain taxes and other financial responsibilities, individually, for each location.

Growing your business, in various forms, should be an end goal for every 'Broke Entrepreneur'. Utilize your time and resources to expand. Always remember to remember the sacrifices you made to be an entrepreneur and the sacrifices you may continue to make. Ensure that when your children, family members, or friends want to open a business, they will not have to start off as a 'Broke Entrepreneur' due to finances. However, teach them how to have a 'Broke Entrepreneur' mindset; exploring monetary and non-monetary options for success. Assist them with sustaining their business as they become an 'Assertive Entrepreneur'.

You will start your business as a 'Broke Entrepreneur.' However, the work you put into your business will allow you to be able to provide options for your family, friends, and others who are budding entrepreneurs. Your success may allow you to be in a position where you are a funder, partner, or potential investor assisting a 'Broke Entrepreneur' with following their dreams. I pride myself on being a 'Broke Entrepreneur'. It reminds me of the steps I took that enabled me to go beyond that in which I thought I was capable. I continue to explore and keep in mind that my success has no limits. Being a 'Broke Entrepreneur' is not a representation of your end. It represents the beginning of hope, resilience, and determination to believe in yourself, despite a lack of finances. I took a chance. It's your turn 'Broke Entrepreneur'.

References

Shakespeare, Williams. (1885). *The Tragedy of Julius Caesar*. Clarendon Press.

Author's Bio

Tashayla Williams holds a BA in Sociology, BA in Criminal Justice, and a Masters in Mental Health Counseling. Tashayla Williams is currently a Doctor in Philosophy Candidate in Counselor Education and Supervision-Counseling and Social Change. Tashayla is a Nationally Certified Counselor and a Licensed Clinical Professional Counselor.

Tashayla has worked with several populations. Tashayla has worked with abused and neglected teenagers, teenagers transitioning from the juvenile justice system back into society, individuals with disabilities, individuals suffering with co-occurring disorders (mental health and addictions), sex offenders and returning citizens (ex-offenders). Tashayla has also worked with individuals, couples and groups.

Tashayla is a person-centered therapist who provides psychotherapy and expressive art and music therapy in private practice, jail, and prison settings. Tashayla is the founder of Life Embodied Therapy LLC and the developer of the Offender To Returning Citizen-Transition Program.